Table Flowers

Table Flowers

Over 50 Arrangements for Simple, Special and Spectacular Occasions

Shane Connolly

photography by Jan Baldwin

With all love for my parents Gerry and Peggy Connolly
and my wife Candida

First published in 1996 by
Conran Octopus Limited
a part of the Octopus Publishing Group
2–4 Heron Quays
London E14 4JP
www.conran-octopus.co.uk

Reprinted 1996
This paperback edition published 2002

Commissioning Editor: Louise Simpson
Senior Editor: Jenna Jarman

Art Editor: Leslie Harrington
Stylist: Lucinda Egerton
Typesetter: Olivia Norton

Production Controller: Julia Golding
Indexer: Indexing Specialists

British Library Cataloguing-in-Publication Data
A catalogue record for this book is available from the British Library.

ISBN 1 84091 295 2
Printed in China

Contents

Introduction 6

Simple 9

**Uncomplicated ideas for every day.
Casual meals made special with simple, quick
and unpretentious arrangements.**

Entertaining 55

**Ideas for small gatherings.
Flowers set the scene for relaxed dinners, fun-themed
parties or exquisite evenings to remember.**

Celebrations 99

**Entertaining on a large scale.
Memorable flowers for the special occasions
in life, from weddings and christenings
to anniversaries and festive parties.**

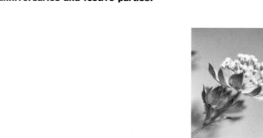

MY CAREER IN FLOWERS is founded on a life-long fascination with nature and any growing thing. This is inevitably reflected in a generally unstructured 'style' of using cut flowers or plants for decoration. I also find that flowers which at least look like they might have seen a field or garden in their brief life are more appealing than any cosseted, exotic flower-shop treasure. There are exceptions – when the setting or occasion demands a more stylized effect – but even these can be approached from a natural perspective.

The term 'natural' is much used and abused by flower arrangers. Often arrangements have to include several colours, ten varieties and a dozen terracotta pots to qualify. To me, a natural approach to flowers is primarily one based upon an instinctive response to the flower itself. I therefore prefer to use just a few types of seasonal flowers simply, with the prime objective of showing them off and emphasizing their individual characteristics.

The great joy of table arrangements – especially in the setting of a home – is that they allow one to emphasize the beauty of the flowers rather than the skill of the fashion-conscious arranger. It is not at all like designing for grand rooms or large spaces, where the arranger has to resort to feats of mechanical genius to hold a towering arrangement together. No, the table is a much simpler and more

welcoming canvas, and available flowers and foliage can easily be a starting point. A suitable setting built up around them with careful choice of cloth, container and china then shows them off to their best advantage. Rarer or more delicate flowers, such as widow irises or hellebores, whose subtlety makes them unsuited to large displays, can be kept in smaller quantities and enjoyed from a close vantage point.

Generally, I prefer to use natural-looking, seasonal flowers in table decorations, which is why in this book I often choose garden rather than shop varieties. This keeps the much-needed excitement and spontaneity alive and, theoretically, means one uses flowers at their strongest and best. I am also fond of using growing plants on tables whenever possible, as they have an aura of simplicity and unpretentiousness that suits most everyday tables. And even on the most formal celebratory tables, growing ingredients can afterwards provide unique and lasting mementoes.

Light also has a significant effect on my choice of flowers. Harsh summer light makes vibrant mixtures rather aggressive, while soft spring light makes equally vivid narcissi look cheerful and glowing. Blue, for instance, looks magical in daylight yet sickly in artificial light, so blue flowers are usually reserved for breakfast or lunch tables where they can remain fresh and unsullied. Bear in mind, then, the effect of candle or electric light on flowers, and experiment with tones and shades to find which blooms suit your lighting.

You also need to take space and practical considerations into account: remember that table flowers are usually seen from all sides. You should not obscure the guests' views of each other with tall flowers – no matter how tempting this is sometimes – yet I feel that tall flowers can work and are in fact essential for breaking the monotony of flat party tables. If you do want to use tall flowers, make sure they are above eye level, or position arrangements at either end of a long table or at one side of a square table, with seats only on the other three sides. Be bold, experiment and think only of making the table look good from the angles at which it will be seen.

I try to choose flowers to suit their setting, so it looks natural for them to be there. Flowers for the everyday table at home are most successful when they reflect the taste of the person who lives there and fit their surroundings, rather than bend to the dictates of the floral style gurus. Flowers, containers, china, tablecloth and cutlery are interdependent within their setting, and say something about who you are. In the section entitled Simple there are examples of fresh, unaffected ways of using flowers with everyday china and objects.

Flowers for special meals or supper parties bring with them their own rules and personalities, allowing you to pursue wild themes or a new style for a while. I have tried to include the thematic and

dramatic approach to small special table arrangements in the section called Entertaining. Sometimes these may be more expensive options, but they will always make a memorable impact on your guests.

The section entitled Celebrations was devised with those familiar special occasions in mind – largely weddings, christenings and anniversaries, where flowers are often needed in large quantities. Here I have tried to show how you can still do really wonderful things without taking out a second mortgage. Designs have been created with the idea that you may need 10, 20 or even 30 of them to fill your guests' tables. Cost and practical considerations, such as the longevity of the flowers, are then as important as your overall theme.

Whichever style of table arranging you choose, always try to approach flower arranging with a certain lightheartedness. These works of art are transient and, by nature, imperfect, so don't be too serious about the more unsuccessful attempts. There should be no rules for the imagination. To borrow the words of Constance Spry:

Do what you please, follow your own star; be oriental if you want to be and don't if you don't want to be. Just be natural and gay and light-hearted and pretty and simple and overflowing and general and baroque and austere and stylized and wild and daring and conservative and learn and learn. Open your minds to every form of beauty.

Simple

**Flaring tulips on a
sprightly checked cloth.**

*A tapestry of garden
roses for afternoon tea.*

**Rich fruits and berries to
brighten autumn suppers.**

*Green pears and
golden leaves glistening
at Christmas.*

Hyacinths

MOTHER'S DAY LUNCH

Pale hyacinths are both pretty and contemporary when grouped *en masse* for this Mother's Day lunch.

The cut flowers were bought a few days before and allowed to 'open' for maximum scent and impact, before being simply arranged with some shortened stems of cultivated guelder. The container is home-made: a frosted glass bowl firmly glued to a matching upturned bonbon dish. The useful result will add height and delicacy to many arrangements; these stocky hyacinths seem to lighten considerably as they flow gently over the edges of the bowl. The delicate guelder roses soften the effect further while their limey colour, along with the plain green frosted glassware, both frames and freshens the pastel tones. For another occasion they could be arranged even more simply in a row of frosted glasses. Either way, hyacinths make very long-lasting cut flowers – especially when arranged without their own foliage.

A mouthwatering combination of heady scents – hyacinth and fresh melon – make an enticing lunch table on a wet spring Sunday. The colours were inspired by the translucent pastels of glâcé fruits – seen above with similar frosted glassware – and are framed to perfection by the soft lemon tablecloth and limey green guelder roses *(Viburnum opulus)*.

Widow Iris

A STYLISH DINNER

Yet both so passing strange and wonderful

P.B. SHELLEY (1792–1822)

The curious blooms of the widow iris *(Hermodactylus tuberosus)* with Turkish chincherinchees *(Ornithogalum arabicum)* in a contemporary city apartment. Their subtle colours and unusual markings can be appreciated fully against the serene white walls.

For a very few weeks in late winter the strangely modest blooms of the widow iris are available as cut flowers.

Despite being short lived, they are cheap, delicately scented and guaranteed to cause a stir. For this particular setting, I wanted to arrange them in a fairly natural way, and these curved vases, with a gun-metal glaze, proved ideal to hold the stems in vertical clumps, as if growing. The greeny whites of Turkish chincherinchees, in a warmer pottery vase, created a centre point in the overall elliptical design, and prevented the whole from becoming too stark.

Finding the right setting for flowers with such quirky and delicate coloration is quite tricky, as they can easily be upstaged by brighter flowers. If you need to mix them, try the simple elegance of white camellias or sweetly scented white narcissi. Personally, though, I think they are at their best on their own, left to cast their cool, quiet spell over a simple modern table.

An invigorating blend of ruby red Japanese quince (*Chaenomeles*) and the pinkish-red camellia 'Black Lace' tumble casually from an etched green glass bowl in a simple, warm spring arrangement.

Camellias

LUNCH À DEUX

Spring is the season of many floral treats and camellias are one of its earliest surprises.

A few branches of camellia and chaenomeles, with buds beginning to open, were cut and arranged in a jug of water indoors to allow the flowers to unfold gradually, protected from possible frost or rain damage. When both had started to flower inside, it was simplicity itself to cut some shapely sprays of each to decorate an impromptu lunch table. The green etched glass enhances the Japanese feeling of both flowers, while its leafy colour frames their redness. Such arrangements are always best if they look casual – place stems for balance rather than any definite shape and accept the first, most natural, attempt rather than overhandling and over-arranging. Other similar early garden performers that suit this 'unarranged' look include the fragrant daphne (*Daphne odora*), wintersweet (*Chimonanthus praecox*), Chinese witch hazel (*Hamamelis mollis*) and several early fruit blossoms.

Snowdrops

VALENTINE'S DINNER

Clumps of snowdrops make an enchanting alternative to red roses for this Saint Valentine's day table.

Looking deceptively established in an aluminium cake ring, they were in fact carefully dug up, in flower, from the garden. It is important not to damage the bulbs nor disturb the soil and roots too much when you do this. Fortunately, snowdrops seem to transplant best when green rather than in their dormant bulb state, so these clumps, replanted directly into the ring shape with extra soil added, were unperturbed by their ordeal. To finish off, gravel seemed a more contemporary choice than moss, and it succeeds in drawing attention to the amazing sleekness of these elegant early bulbs.

Presented like this, snowdrops can also make an inexpensive and novel engagement gift. Alternatively, you can easily buy small pots of various spring bulbs that could be planted in a similar way.

An auspicious ring of crisp snowdrops decorates a small table, taking on a surprisingly urbane air with their plain metal container and edging of cool gravel. A ring cake tin, such as this, should prove useful – whatever the long-term prospects of the romantic diners!

Crocus

FUN LUNCH

Simplicity, combined with youthful freshness, makes an easy winner out of this long-lasting arrangement.

During spring, flowering bulbs are available in the shops. These common-or-garden purple crocus were bought in tight bud, removed from their plastic pots and replanted into this circular galvanized tray. Any container has potential and junk stores often yield unexpected treasures. It is best to use an inner plastic bowl or a sheet of polythene to give your container a waterproof lining, while a handful of stones also helps with drainage. The bulbs are then planted and the surface is covered with small helxine plants (moss, stones, gravel or even tiny shells would also look pretty). Most bulbs should be kept moist but not wet and it is important to water them over a sink to avoid damage to furniture. This sort of arrangement remains a joy over several weeks and can then be recycled straight into the garden to flower again year after year.

The vibrant purple of growing crocus underplanted with the sharp lime of mind-your-own-business (Helxine) looks clean and fresh with a checked cloth and brightly coloured china. The flowers open at dawn and close at dusk and are therefore most pleasing for daylight meals, when they can be enjoyed at every stage from the emerging buds to their final fading and delicate wrinkling.

These purple crocus seem particularly vivacious and bright in their contemporary setting. Conversely, cream crocus would look understated and serene in a softly patterned china bowl, their extraordinarily sensual satin texture offset by a satin or damask cloth. Also try sunshine yellow crocus on shocking pink satin – to steal the show at a fun party or breathe life into a characterless marquee.

Hellebores
GOING DUTCH

A conglomeration of garden gems was gathered in the long dull days of winter and illustrates perfectly the much

underestimated pleasures of winter-flowering plants – even the smallest garden should contain some winter performers. The only rule for creating this sort of table is that such rare treasures should be properly conditioned to ensure that they last as long as possible. (The only 'problem' plants here are the hellebores, but they last wonderfully if conditioned as described on page 124.) Lenten roses display an amazing range of subtle shades, and the blotchy purple-pink ones used here inspired me to emulate a sort of Dutch still-life on this wine-coloured cloth. The classically shaped containers range from small antique glasses to tall decanters, and the height does not interfere with the meal as the seating is arranged on three sides only. Such an eclectic display can be repeated with infinite variation through the seasons.

Informal garden flowers make a relaxing still-life and a talking point for supper with fellow enthusiasts. The flowers include Lenten roses (*Helleborus orientalis, H. corsicus* and *H. foetidus*), camellia, the marbled leaves of an *Arum italicum*, *Rhododendron* 'Christmas Cheer', *Daphne odora* and *Iris* 'Pauline'.

Auriculas

AN INFORMAL DINNER

Fastidious persons,
Epicurean Puritans
Of reserved vision
Meticulous in decision
Cherish the Auricula

From an Arabic poem translated by
SIR CHARLES LYALL

Auriculas in colours of an exquisite old Aubusson rug are mounded in a marble mortar. These aristocratic cousins of the common primula are often distinguished by a powdery white coating, which enhances their subtle faded appeal.

Fragrant auriculas have been the subject of several revivals through history –

perhaps most notably in the seventeenth century, when plants reportedly fetched £20 each among enthusiasts! This arrangement was inspired by a painting of about 1600 by Jacques Linard, which depicts not growing auriculas but cut stems massed in a small basket. Perhaps this was merely one plantsman's fantasy, but it has a beauty I longed to copy. I bought several plants, cut the flowers off low down near the soil level and simply arranged them in the container in fresh water. This sounds wasteful, but the plants are unharmed and live to bloom another day. This old marble mortar has a patina similar to auriculas, and the combination, with powdery figs, is my idea of heaven. A few plants would look almost as exquisite planted in this bowl – albeit more diluted with leaves and stems. Do try auriculas – cut or growing – in stone or metal containers too, or in the ever-reliable old terracotta pots.

Double Primroses
SPRING TEA

A clutch of pale double primroses, their mass of fluffy and frivolous heads held tightly in a wire basket, is a pretty adornment for afternoon tea. The mood is light and fresh, and the colours echo the medley of primrosy china and lemon-checked cloth.

This tea table is particularly pleasing because the impact relies on a thoughtful blend

of flowers and tableware, rather than hours of preparation and effort. So many small outdoor plants can now be bought in a state of flowering perfection that it seems a shame not to enjoy them inside first. These double primroses were unpotted and placed with some soil in a green metal container, which fitted within the basket. All that remained was to neaten the surface with a decorative layer of moss. As with the growing bulb decorations shown earlier in the book, the choice of container is limitless as long as it can be made fairly watertight. Equally, these plants should not be overwatered and should be replanted outside in a week or so. Any pretty plant is suitable for such treatment: primulas or violas look enchanting with flowery china, tiny roses make pretty miniature rose gardens and bedding plants like petunias, nicotianas and geraniums make ideal visitors at a casual dining table.

Ranunculus

SQUARE MEALS

Creating different moods does not necessarily depend upon a vast store of vases,

china and tablecloths. This cheap and jolly tablecloth, with some basic china, is the setting for three meals – each with a very different ambience created by simple, well-considered flowers. The wire basket had a snugly fitting small bowl inside for water and flowers, and the fabric was twisted around this before arranging them.

In the main photograph the feeling is one of youthful lightheartedness, with the colourful ranunculus picking out almost every colour in the cloth. Emerson once said that the earth 'laughs in flowers' and these cheery, up-market relatives of the buttercup certainly bring a smile. A turquoise lining would also look effective.

The lilac table with its subtle green silk is altogether calmer and almost old-fashioned with the gentler colours and sweet lilac scent. This contrasts with the third, more contemporary arrangement, with bold yellow silk and dark purple violets proclaiming a stylish confidence.

Top: **Pale lilac with *eau-de-nil* silk for a calm and feminine look.**

Above: **Scented violets with yellow silk combines two strong colours with drama.**

Right: **Cheery ranunculus with lipstick–pink silk imitate the vivid freshness of the tablecloth, whose bright and colourful checks inspired me to do three variations on a theme.**

Blazing Tulips

DINNER WITH FRIENDS

Sometimes, because of the decor or the occasion, subtle flowers are not appropriate.

In this busy room, every cheerful colour vies for attention and only bold flowers can survive, so I opted for hot orange, red and pink tulips, which would draw out the colours of the patchwork but be strong enough to be noticed and admired by guests. I also mixed tulips of different shapes to keep the display fairly informal – this works particularly well for casual surroundings, where 'smart' uniform stems would strike the wrong note.

I also took care to ensure that the flowers were placed in groups of one colour and were carried through in patterns of tone, rather than being dotted singly about the arrangement. This is especially important when you are dealing with bright colours, which appear bitty and disappointingly dull if they are diluted with too much green or other hues. Unfortunately, such flower-intensive arrangements usually have to be kept for more special occasions, as they can end up being quite expensive.

A blazing bouquet of massed tulips – singles, doubles, parrots and Aladdin types – in flaming shades of pinks, oranges and reds. Set on an equally irrepressible old silk patchwork used as a tablecloth, they create a feisty table for dinner.

Constance Spry advised that, when arranging a single type of flower, it was important to emphasize some aspect or attribute of that flower in its natural growing state. It is interesting to contrast these tulips with those shown on page 105, which are arranged with a lighter touch to show off the wonderfully sinuous shapes of the growing stems. Here, however, I have set out to do something different. This bolder display tries instead to capture the impact of tulips growing *en masse* in Dutch fields with that impression of concentrated colour devoid of green.

Lily-of-the-Valley

MAY-DAY LUNCH

Who art so lovely fair and smell'st so sweet

That the sense aches at thee   SHAKESPEARE (1564–1616)

Simple and delicate – a few stems of sweet-smelling lily-of-the-valley in an old French hand-painted ink-pot, or in stylish formation (arranged without leaves) in small recycled glass bottles. Either way, lilies-of-the-valley are a treat for the senses with their exquisite fragrance and perfect prettiness.

The French have a delightful custom of giving friends lilies-of-the-valley (*muguets*) on May Day. On the first of May you see the small scented bunches on sale everywhere – even in the Métro stations, allowing commuters to pick up a small token of spring in the middle of the rush hour.

These cut stems of lily-of-the-valley need to be put into water immediately. Crushing the bottom few centimetres of stem helps them drink, and placing them in quite warm water often revives the more reluctant bought bunch. Like many exquisite spring flowers, I prefer to arrange them simply and alone – they do not belong to the voluptuous mixed borders of summer – so I choose small-necked containers that allow them to be arranged delicately, much as they grow in the garden.

This old ink-pot makes a charming holder for a few stems – rather like one of Fabergé's bejewelled flower creations. Alternatively, the small glass bottles, formally arranged in a square group, make a stronger, cleaner display for a contemporary setting.

Roses

SUMMER SUPPER

The cool colours of this mosaic bowl blend perfectly with the blue-grey foliage

of rue, sedum and echeveria, and creamy white roses – all picked from the garden in midsummer. This is flower arranging at its most enjoyable – choosing a container and filling it with flowers picked from the garden. Alternatively, wander first and select the container later. As always, the flowers were well conditioned before arranging – especially important with any garden roses, as they last much longer if properly treated.

There are a host of garden flowers that we often forget when it comes to arranging, such as echeveria – that familiar grey rosette-shaped succulent – which is easily grown and gives such good texture and interest here. Moreover, it is worth noting how a few beautiful flowers can be enhanced with the addition of interesting bits and pieces. This is especially useful with shop-bought flowers, which are vastly improved and naturalized by a complement of garden foliage.

The beautifully scented climbing rose 'Madame Alfred Carrière', supplemented with glaucous foliage, fennel, and unripened edible miniature strawberries (*fraises des bois*), spills out from a pretty mosaic bowl to make this dreamy table arrangement. Simple linen and china ensure that the sumptuous flowers are kept centre stage.

White Roses

A STYLISH TABLE

Owners of modern homes usually choose flowers that are just as up-to-the-minute,

such as sunflowers and lilies. 'Old-fashioned' flowers, however, can cast a more subtle spell in a modern setting, providing you choose simple, structural containers and opt for strongly architectural designs. Here I have chosen a wonderfully solid old marble mortar and simply piled the cut, conditioned stems of the rose 'Glamis Castle' into it without any trace of foliage. Some may balk at the idea of removing a flower's foliage, but it can be highly effective. Here the rose's delicate pearl colours are emphasized strongly, yet any tendency to over-prettiness is avoided. Similarly, the sprays of an old *wichuraiana* hybrid rose have a chance to show off their exquisite structure of florets and wiry branching stems when arranged singly in glass oil bottles like botanical specimens. A row of these bottles could be equally striking on a long table and, provided they were tall enough, would not interfere with your guests' view.

An old marble mortar heaped with the creamy scented cups of the English rose 'Glamis Castle', with three contemporary oil jars – each holding one stem of an old *wichuraiana* hybrid rose – standing sentinel around it. A harmonious blend of old and new in a thoroughly modern setting.

Garden Foliage

ALFRESCO LUNCH

Verdant green and gold foliage of every hue makes up this garden table decoration. The effect is one of cool, relaxing informality, ideal for a lunch table under a hot sun.

A foliage arrangement makes a refreshing change for an early-summer table.

At this stage in the growing year, leaves are still vibrantly healthy – not yet touched by the ravages of hot, dry days – and a joy to use. I have chosen a glorious medley of hosta leaves, variegated astrantias, euphorbias, fennel, lemon balm and unripe blackcurrants. Golden philadelphus (*P. coronarius* 'Aureus'), honeysuckle and feverfew add the only touches of flower. First everything was cut and conditioned the day before and left in a bucket of water. I then arranged the leaves in this lovely old pea-green painted terracotta bowl, letting the stems follow their natural contours. It is worth painting a few cheap bowls and leaving them outside for a while to acquire that subtle patina so flattering to most flowers.

This table arrangement, while perhaps not as dainty as the previous two, shows that a carefully chosen selection of scented greenness, without flower, is certainly not dull and is a perfect choice for a lush garden setting.

Old Roses

AFTERNOON TEA

For thousands of years the rose has been among the most prized of the flowers we cultivate in our gardens.

Throughout the world it has been exalted in art and literature and, in the last century, was grown and hybridized almost out of recognition. These old roses seem to capture, even in their beautiful names, a hint of that more ancient past. They are best cut just as the flowers open rather than in bud and then conditioned immediately. Put them in a container with water (and chicken wire if necessary) rather than floral foam and try to cluster the flower heads together as here, so that you emphasize their naturally voluptuous qualities.

Roses are an appropriate choice when entertaining friends and family, as they symbolize secrecy and mystery. Back in the Middle Ages, they were hung from ceilings to indicate the confidentiality of conversations – a custom continuing in plaster ceiling roses even today.

Traditional and timeless – a silver bowl of old garden roses. *Rosa* 'Henri Martin', 'Louise Odier', 'Chapeau de Napoléon', *Rosa officinalis, R. mundi*, 'Old Blush China' and 'La Reine Victoria', with a few stems of honeysuckle, herb robert (*Geranium robertianum*) and red valerian (*Centranthus ruber*) softening their solidity.

English Roses

BREAKFAST FOR TWO

Scented English roses, their subtle colours accentuated by purple-hued flowers and foliage, in an old plant pot.

This table display is in many ways the antithesis of the preceding rose arrangement, suggesting soft-toned restraint rather than rich voluptuousness. Again however, the flowers have been complemented by garden foliage, and the use of light and dark materials creates a sort of floral *chiaroscuro*. I particularly liked the old square terracotta pot, with its dusty white patina, which complements the buff shades of *Rosa* 'Cymbeline' and flatters its soft texture so perfectly. The foliage also presents a dramatic range of hues – from rich aubergine to deep sepia – effectively bringing out the slightly purply tones of *R.* 'Charles Rennie Mackintosh' and making these special blooms go much further. Strange hues are well worth experimenting with – the results are both eye-catching and satisfying.

The unique and exquisite ashen shades of the English roses 'Cymbeline' and 'Charles Rennie Mackintosh' set a quiet note of subtlety in an old square French plant pot. Creamy penstemon, purple sage, astrantia, dark purple-black alliums and leaves of *Heuchera* 'Palace Purple' frame the blooms.

All Blues

SUMMER LUNCH

High summer is often a dull time for flowers. Nothing is at its best and the only flowers you can buy in quantity are lilies and chrysanthemums. This is often a good time to use a collection of containers that each hold only one or two stems of the remaining precious garden flowers. The overall effect is then one of abundance, especially if you choose flowers of a similar colour and continue this through your containers and tableware. Here I have chosen flowers in all shades of blue – one of my personal favourites – and used an odd assortment of old blue glass bottles in similar colours. Blue flowers look best in natural light, as their colours are truer than when under electric light. This makes them ideal for decorating a breakfast or lunch table, when natural light will show off their intense colours to best advantage.

Bottles like this can be found very cheaply on market stalls and in jumble sales and are very useful for tables, mantelpieces and anywhere a collection of flowers can be displayed. Contemporary bottles, like those on page 35, are equally useful and really help to show off individual flowers – almost like botanical illustrations. Group them informally or arrange similar bottles in elegant patterns, like the lily-of-the-valley arrangement on page 30.

Strong cobalt-blue glassware and linen make the perfect setting for an azurine collection of blue and purple flowers delicately arranged in an assortment of old bottles. Flowers include sweet peas, agapanthus, lavender, cornflowers, penstemons, eryngium, perovskia, echinops and forget-me-nots.

Gentians with Berries

AUTUMN SUPPER

Autumn is the season of several of nature's most extraordinary experiments in colour coordination.

Clashes that would appear jarring in harsh summer light are rich and brilliant in the gentler light of autumn. In contrast to the glorious masses of one type of flower on spring tables, it seems more appropriate to make rich and opulent mixtures using seasonal fruits, berries and fewer flowers for autumn tables. This vibrant platter is deceptively simple and economical to put together. Two plants of autumn-flowering gentians provided the starting point. I placed them, still with their surrounding soil, on either side of a small bowl of floral foam in this oval pewter platter. Cabbages, fruit and berries were then 'planted' into and around the floral foam, concealing any trace of mechanics. The gentian trails were threaded through the whole arrangement and, with the burgundy chenille cloth, the effect was one of rich abundance.

A sumptuous blend of electric–blue growing gentians with autumnal berries: inky-purple grapes on the vine, privet and viburnum berries, damsons, sloes, elderberries, and the racemes of Virginian pokeweed berries (*Phytolacca americana*) with beetroot leaves and cabbages.

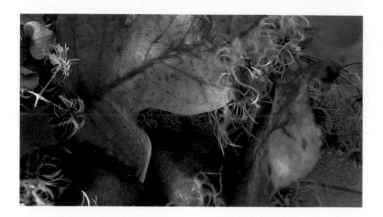

Chestnuts
CLASSICAL TABLE

The earthy ochre and sepia tints of fallen leaves and nuts are the basis of this mellow table arrangement.

As on the preceding page, the richness of the season inspired me to select a mixture of ingredients in these subtle autumn colours, which I felt were complete without the addition of flowers. This meant that water was unnecessary and the construction totally straightforward. I simply piled exquisite mahogany chestnuts with beige-brown dead hydrangea heads (barely visible) to make a basic mound shape in the bowl. This was then softened with trails of wild clematis (the fluffy heads dry easily) and fallen leaves from a tulip tree with their quirky blunt-ended shape.

Autumn walks yield all sorts of wonderful treasures, making free arrangements like these a great seasonal pleasure. Try others based on maple leaves in copper bowls or mixtures of nuts and shells in simple pottery.

A subtle blend of earthy autumnal tones in this elegant stone bowl looks both classical and contemporary. It is simply composed of nature's cast-offs: dead hydrangea heads, chestnuts (both in and out of their prickly green case), vine leaves, trails of wild clematis or old-man's beard (*Clematis vitalba*) and a few shapely golden bronze leaves from the elegant tulip tree (*Liriodendron tulipifera*).

Amaryllis

WINTER BREAKFAST

This clean wintry freshness makes a welcome alternative to the florid sparkles of the Christmas season.

Fully open white amaryllis flowers, with startling citrus centres, were casually mixed with spidery stems of *Cornus mas*; the twigs, with a natural coating of scaly lichen, were brought inside several weeks earlier so their fragrant lemon flowers were already beginning to open. Amaryllis make excellent long-lasting cut flowers, beautiful for weeks if bought in bud. They are seldom used on tables – perhaps because of the intimidating length of bare stem. Try using them in bud in stylish tall arrangements, and when they are fully open, cut them down for low displays like this. It is also a good way of using up straggly limbs of pot-grown amaryllis before the flower weight snaps the stem. The translucent white petals create a calming picture in this pale green room, but the bright pinks, apricots and reds are a wonderful choice for a warmer arrangement.

Luminous white amaryllis flowers arranged in a sleek silver bowl with a few lichen-clad twigs of cornelian cherry (*Cornus mas*).

Golden Pears

CHRISTMAS LUNCH

Inspired by a 15th-century painted garland, this table decoration has an element of Renaissance formality.

A striking and sophisticated Christmas table that takes minutes to create. Fresh pears and gilded skeletonized leaves are simply placed on a cloth of golden metallic organza over rich green silk – perfect for that romantic first Christmas together.

Structurally this arrangement is very simple, as the components are merely placed on the table in a regular pattern of leaves and fruit. Available from dried-flower suppliers, the skeletonized leaves are from a magnolia tree, and are just sprayed lightly with metallic gold paint (fine gold glitter would add extra sparkle but might have fought here with the soft glow of the green silk and organza). Finally, to add texture and depth, I placed some leaves slightly over the fruit and finished each end with an exuberant knot of shimmering organdie ribbon. The possible variations are infinite: black grapes and silver leaves with a purple undercloth would look cool and stylish, while a red cloth with golden organza and leaves would make a traditional complement to pomegranates and cranberries.

Roman Hyacinths

WINTER SUPPER

Using the simplest decorative ingredients often leaves the most memorable impression.

A scented still-life of lemons, both cut and whole, with the glossy citrus-like leaves of Portugal laurel (*Prunus lusitanica*), starry Roman hyacinths and sprigs of rosemary. The cobalt-blue glassware and glazed Mexican bowls complete the rich and homely picture.

This composition, in two pottery bowls, is remarkably cheap to put together: a few stems of Portugal laurel and rosemary, some beautifully shaped Cyprus and Sweet lemons and two bunches of Roman hyacinths with star-shaped flowers resembling lemon blossom. The scented, painterly result gives an exquisite impression of lemons growing with their own foliage and flowers. White narcissi could replace the rarer hyacinths – which are held in place in the water-filled bowl by the lemons and foliage. The lemons are not wired and therefore can be removed and used as needed, so the whole effect is as unarranged as possible. The choice of container should always suit the setting – small urns of lemons and stephanotis would look exquisite in a grander room, for example. I always try to glean ideas for similar combinations of fruit and flowers from early Dutch and Spanish still lifes.

Entertaining

Stately magnolias in a vase of palest stone.

A basket of golden roses on a balmy summer night.

Delicate ropes of hydrangeas evoking aristocratic elegance.

Ethereal mistletoe adding pagan magic to a modern Christmas.

Magnolia

SPRING DINNER PARTY

A few flushed ivory flowers of *Magnolia* x *soulangeana* look rare and exotic in small stone-filled marble bowls placed along a table. The minimalist grandeur of the plant is also highlighted in an arrangement of three branches, which seem to float upon their glass side-table.

Some flowers really need no embellishments – they speak most loudly arranged alone and with unerring simplicity.

The magnolia family are such flowers. They have a stateliness that seems to magnify when cut and used thoughtfully indoors. These early-flowering magnolias escape frost and rain damage when cut in bud and, if arranged carefully without bruising, the flowers can open in the warmth of your home and reach perfection. These particular blooms were carefully anchored in a heavy marble bowl with chicken wire and floral foam. The stones avoid the need for foliage to cover the mechanics and also complement the cool alabaster quality of the flowers themselves. A similar design was used for several smaller bowls on the dining table with only one or two flowers in each. Both lasted many days. Magnolias are one of several shrubs that can be grown in containers and brought inside to flower.

Narcissus
SPRING BIRTHDAY

Bright daffodils and graceful narcissi are some of the first flowers of spring – and widely available as cut flowers. They are notoriously difficult to arrange naturally however, partly because of the straightness of their stems and fullness of trumpet, which can lead to them looking stiff and overcrowded. I prefer to use growing narcissi in their miniature varieties for table decoration. Although they can be planted into all types of containers, the narcissi in this mossy bank are an altogether more exciting approach and extremely simple to copy. First cut a length of strong black polythene to fit the table, place the desired number of pots along it, and cut or fold the polythene to within a few centimetres of the pot. Finally, cover the whole with moss and neaten the edges. It is better not to water the arrangement at all as it is not watertight. Instead, simply plant the bulbs outside when they start to flag.

Being an unpretentious flower, *Narcissus* 'Tête-à-Tête' looks best with simple settings, such as these wooden plates and recycled glass goblets, but its more sophisticated cousin *N.* 'Paper White' is exquisite with linen and silver.

And Narcissi, the fairest of them all,

Who gaze on their eyes in the stream's recess,

Till they die at their own dear loveliness…

P.B. SHELLEY (1792–1822)

A mossy bank of miniature golden narcissi growing along this dark wooden table completes a special birthday meal. This variety, 'Tête-à-Tête', is widely available in early spring. A few bunches of the first primroses in little mismatched containers add to the relaxed charm of this jolly table.

Easter Blossom

DRINKS PARTY

Loveliest of trees, the cherry now
Is hung with bloom along the bough,
And stands about the woodland ride
Wearing white for Easter tide.

A.E. HOUSMAN (1859–1936)

Boughs of white blossom are the epitome of spring in this minimalist city-centre flat – their height is appropriate for a drinks party and the blossom will stay in view even when the room is full of guests.

The natural simplicity of this arrangement is perfect for such an airy, modern space, filled with pale furnishings and city decor.

Flower shops are gradually realizing the value of simple flowers and now one can often buy bunches of blossom, forsythia, catkins and other willowy branches in their season. They make perfect decorations for large airy spaces and need minimal arranging. These single blossoms are best bought, or cut, in bud so that when handling them you are less likely to damage the delicate petals. This also gives the added pleasure of watching them open and the whole arrangement slowly come to life. Remember that these branches are heavy – make sure your chicken wire or floral foam is firmly attached to its bowl before arranging and try not to think of a 'shape' as you arrange, but let the direction of each branch follow its own natural course. The tiny nests were made by shaping some moss by hand and binding it with fine wire. An arrangement like this, held high by the stem on the bowl, need not obscure vision for seated guests, but it is obviously better suited to buffet and drinks tables. Double blossoms look even more dramatic, albeit slightly prettier and more traditional. Try some pink blossom in an old Chinese bowl for a less contemporary setting, or double white blossom in an old iron or marble urn for a majestic spring wedding buffet.

Far left: **These delicate racemes of blossom are from the stems of bird cherry (*Prunus padus*) at the front of the arrangement.**

Right: **The contemporary wooden Japanese bowl emphasizes the undeniably oriental ambience that blossom creates. The height of the blossom leaves the table surface clear for party food and these charming nests of moss, filled with painted chocolate eggs.**

Clematis

BUSINESS LUNCH

Clematis montana is one of nature's most rampant and invasive ruffians.

Then, in spring, it transforms itself into a refined and generous flowering beauty, which may be cut with impunity as flowers are plentiful and the blooms keep well in water. It is also well worth bringing indoors, as its short season obliges you to make the most of it. This plant, however, is so appreciative of its own beauty that it clings passionately to itself and you need to be patient to free several long trails. The flowers here were cut just as buds were opening. A tall vase or piece of furniture generally shows off *Clematis montana* best and most naturally. This vase may seem extreme for a table but, placed at one side, it does not obscure your view. More importantly, it also works as a main room decoration and continues to look good for the rest of the working day, unlike many table arrangements that seem out of place once the meal is over. Trails of roses or hops snaking from a tall vase could create a similar effect.

A tall vase of pale blue Mexican glass like this one makes the perfect container for trails of pink *Clematis montana* – bringing a delicate touch of drama to this business lunch and transforming an uninspiring office.

Summer Lilac

SUNDAY LUNCH

This comfortable and unpretentious table, with its harmonious blending of blues, lilacs and purples, homely china and sandy yellow cloth, sets the scene for a tranquil Sunday afternoon with family and friends. The style of arrangement is equally relaxed, with mounds of lilac flowers throwing their warm, heady scent across the table for all to appreciate. The flowers, having first been well conditioned the night before, are casually heaped into two soup tureens and a stemmed bowl. You do need quite a lot of lilac, however, as the stems were stripped of foliage to make them last longer and show off the blooms to their full glory. Texture and variety were introduced with clumps of the broccoli-like double muscari and, in the middle bowl, some bluebells add height. Clematis and daintier flowers soften the outline and give a central focus.

All that calm Sunday that goes on and on.

J.E. FLECKER (1884–1915)

Blue and purple flowers arranged without foliage may not be a novel idea, but, whatever the style or setting, the interplay of natural light through translucent petals of these colours always creates an unparalleled magical brightness, guaranteed to make an impact.

A table laid for an old-fashioned leisurely Sunday lunch. The traditional yellow dining room and pale lemon cloth are the perfect setting for mismatched antique blue-and-white china and an array of early-summer flowers. Generous quantities of scented lilac in several shades of amethyst and bluey lavender are blended with double muscari (*Muscari comosum* 'Plumosum'), the last bluebells, the first cornflower-blue geraniums, azure clematis, chives and a faded purple rhododendron.

Sweet Peas
DRINKS PARTY

Sweet peas are a perennial favourite. Their exquisite scent is matched only by their extraordinary permutations of colour, combining to make a scented 'gown' which is literally breathtaking. Constance Spry recommended that they should be grouped in colours rather than mixed randomly and, following that principle, the sweet peas here were arranged by colour in pastel glass champagne flutes. Surprisingly, the result is clean and elegant. Part of this elegance lies in the delicate twists of the stems clearly visible through the glass and the minimalism of the arrangement: overly generous bowlfuls veer towards the frilly bathing cap school of floristry! Commercial sweet peas do last longer than home-grown ones but they also have the disadvantages of a fainter scent and a complete absence of leaves, tendrils and the general cascading quality of garden sweet peas. Try to recreate these appealing garden qualities if you are using commercial sweet peas by adding trails of delicate greenery – or by using something like this intricate candelabra, which imitates spidery tendrils so magnificently.

Here are sweet peas on tip-toe for a flight,
With wings of gentle flush o'er delicate white,
And taper fingers catching at all things,
To bind them all about with tiny rings.

JOHN KEATS (1795–1821)

Gentle sweet peas, elegantly unadorned, stand to attention in coloured glass champagne flutes. Their long stems and entwining tendrils find echoes in a delicate wire candelabra by British artist Tom Morgan.

Yellow Roses

DINNER ALFRESCO

Blowsy roses, fine wine and good company – the perfect recipe for a relaxed summer evening under the stars.

Won't you come into my garden?
I would like my roses to see you.

R.B. SHERIDAN (1751–1816)

An old basket filled with the English roses 'Golden Celebrations', 'Charlotte' and 'English Garden' on a simply laid garden table. The rich yellows developed in these blooms by breeder David Austin are a shade rarely found in old roses and blend harmoniously with the wild corydalis on the walls behind.

These roses have been arranged to look as if they were simply snipped and laid straight into the basket. They were in fact cut in the coolest part of the previous day and conditioned: each stem being split and placed in a bucket of fresh deep water, allowing them to gather strength so that they last much longer. They were then arranged into a low bowl of pre-soaked floral foam placed in the basket.

Table flowers in a garden setting should blend with rather than distract from their surroundings. The simple basket of roses and the wooden table, with its pretty cloth, hurricane lanterns and plain old china, offer no jarring note in a garden of rustic simplicity. It is also a pleasant conversation point if you are lucky enough to be able to show off flowers from your own garden – or at least choose something that looks as though it may have done!

Strawberries

A SMART PICNIC

A table of sweet-scented philadelphus and miniature strawberries on a hillside…

A ravishing combination of highly scented mock orange (*Philadelphus* 'Belle Etoile' and *P.* 'Burfordensis') and sprays of ripe *fraises des bois* – edible miniature strawberries – make an unforgettable picnic table on a grassy hillside.

Why be practical when one can be utterly self-indulgent? I make no apologies for the inclusion of this pastoral idyll, as it illustrates perfectly that a simple table can be as memorable as a sophisticated extravaganza. Another homemade compote – this time a glass bowl glued on to a sturdy glass candlestick – makes a suitably delicate container for a cloud of single-flowered philadelphus. Like the lilac on page 67, the stems have been stripped of foliage so that the flowers last longer and are more prominent. Then, in a rare red and white combination, I added sprays of alpine strawberries (*fraises des bois*) to echo the embroidered strawberries on the white cloth. These home-grown plants supply an excellent harvest of delicious berries and their decorative sprays are ideal for arranging. No garden should be without them. The result – with pretty china and a prettier view – is the stuff of dreams.

Delphinium and Hollyhock

A COOL LUNCH

A chic combination of almost black and white flowers creates a cool and pretty luncheon table with the hollyhock 'Black Prince', agapanthus, delphiniums, nicotianas and scabious.

An arrangement of flowers that involves strong contrasts needs careful handling, but perhaps none more so than when it involves black and white. Here the extraordinary black-hued hollyhock 'Black Prince' is teamed with white flowers including delphiniums, nicotianas and scabious. They form a host of graduated shades of white, cream, lime-white and green that softens the potential harshness of black with white alone. Only one long stem each of hollyhock and delphinium was used – conditioned first and then cut down into manageable sections. I chose a simple white-painted vase for a centrepiece, with grey-tinted glass tumblers of white agapanthus – again a single stem cut down – around it. A pattern of containers can be made to suit any table shape. As with the previous table, the slightly unusual use of monochromes is carried through to the cloth, embroidered with bugs, and the delightful mock-botanical china. Altogether, a clean and refreshing table for an elegant lunch on a hot summer's day.

Lotus Blossom

AN INDIAN DINNER

I' the East my pleasure lies

SHAKESPEARE (1564–1616)

A jewel-like table reflecting the riches of India, with zinnia and marigold heads floating in marble bowls, the orange-red nasturtium 'Empress of India' in brass pots, and tall lotus flowers towering above thin garlands of exquisitely scented tuberose (*Polianthes tuberosa*).

It is always fascinating to adopt and adapt elements of other cultures into flower decorations. In southern India flowerheads, bereft of stem, are sold by the pound weight. This rather limits their usage to garlands and leis. Bearing this in mind, I set out to decorate a table *à la Indienne* using only flowerheads, but immediately transgressed when I saw these striking lotus flowers (*L. orem ipsem plantum*) making one of their rare market appearances. Using them as a centre point – held high above eye level in a rusty Indian iron container – I proceeded to build up a picture of marble 'ponds', with floating zinnias and marigolds in vibrant clashing colours and a pot or two of nasturtiums emphasizing the hot orange tones. Finishing touches were the scented candles and garlands of fragrant tuberose flowers – the latter simply threaded one by one with a needle and cotton and trailed across the table. Alternatively, one could make circular leis from larger flowerheads for guests to wear around their necks.

Whitecurrants

SUMMER DRINKS PARTY

A gloriously quirky topiary of whitecurrants, greengages, damsons and sedums makes an amusing focal point for a formal garden drinks party.

Currants have an exquisite jewel-like translucence which is irresistibly decorative.

Here I chose whitecurrants to counterpoint the glaucous foliage of sedums and the grey-bloomed skins of greengages. Currants are quite fiddly to use in flower decorations, but when plentiful it is a shame not to enjoy looking at them before making preserves. These generous clusters were secured to a cone of floral foam (bought ready shaped) with hairpins of wire. I then added shapely clumps of sedum and small sprays of greengage and damson – with foliage removed – to punctuate the pyramid of currants. This could look equally beautiful in a sparkling crystal tazza or on a bed of leaves, but this lovely iron urn seemed the perfect container in this formal garden of clipped yews and architectural stonework. Equally tempting would be rich blackcurrants or dramatic redcurrants. Try them heaped in a beautiful bowl for less formal settings or cut on the branch for larger edible arrangements.

Cacti

A SHARP TABLE

A collection of cacti planted in stone-effect pots with 'desert' sand make a bold statement on a contemporary table. The Mexican theme continues in the hot colours of napkins and naïve china. Small clay bowls hold individual cacti to give variation in height.

Desert sand, stone pots and miniature cacti combine to create a table with attitude!

Sometimes life calls for a fun table decoration rather than one produced to reflect your exquisite taste. These prickly cacti make a memorable choice, and may well prove to be your longest-lasting table decoration on record! Small cacti plants are readily available at all times of year and, as long as you wear strong gloves, they can be replanted easily into more decorative containers. I grouped these in threes, selecting my plants for shape and size, and potted them up with recommended cactus compost. The silver sand and pieces of gravel frame the plants more effectively than bare soil and blend with the stone-effect pots. Finally, in true desert style, I decided to scatter the cacti randomly along the table, but they could look equally effective in regular patterns. Cacti seemed a good choice with the bare brick walls and rich sunny china, but more classical tables look wonderful with formal rows of lime helxine or green box plants.

Orchids

A JAPANESE DINNER PARTY

Cut orchids are both readily available and long-lasting flowers. Ideal for simple arrangements, they seemed the perfect choice to suggest this table's Japanese ambience. To keep with the simplicity, I made elegant containers by sawing several poles of bamboo into random lengths and binding them together in bunches with strong wire hidden by rope. Into their hollow centres I placed small plastic tubes of water (cut orchids usually arrive in these tubes at market, so ask your florist to get some) and inserted the stems, with green fern, to create a balanced composition. Finally, the beautiful fountain sculpture – an oriental water garden in miniature – added the cooling sounds of water running over smooth pebbles. Small electrical water pumps can be bought to make similar table fountains in stone or glass bowls.

And as a final note, I should add that while such flower arrangements may be inspired by the art of Ikebana, the Westerner can never approach them with the mastery required. They must, like the Indian table on page 80, make no pretence to being anything other than respectful pastiche.

Creamy *Phalaenopsis* orchids and green ming fern are held in vases of bamboo which are placed around a beautiful bronze fountain sculpture by contemporary British artist Sam Wade.

Hydrangeas
A VINTAGE FEAST

Left: **Delicate garlands of autumnal hydrangeas and grey foliage, coiled around sparkling crystal lustre, evoke a bygone elegance. Napkins are tied with bunches of sweet violets.**

Right: **A contemporary approach to the same materials – a verdigris brass platter is simply piled with hydrangeas, plums and euphorbias.**

Very special birthdays or wedding anniversaries provide irresistible opportunities to pull out all the stops. Choose a theme reminiscent of the year being commemorated – in this case, the elegance of the Edwardian era. Flowers and decor need not be exact reproductions of that era: unless you are creating something for a film or theatre, it is better to suggest the period rather than be slavishly authentic. Asparagus fern and carnations might be more appropriate here, but I was actually inspired by the description of a dress in the *Court Journal* for April 1904: 'Mrs W. F. Taylor's gown was grey chiffon... embroidered in long graceful lines with chenille and steel

sequins. The train was of mauve velvet and satin. She carried a bouquet of Parma violets and her ornaments were diamonds.' Immediately a vision of refined elegance was conjured up: long graceful lines of embroidery became sweeping garlands; steel sequins transformed into the autumnal colours of hydrangeas; and Mrs Taylor's diamonds took on a new life as sparkling chandeliers. A dull grey cloth, old china and silver, and the requisite violets complete the picture and give an unmistakable Edwardian aura with colours and styles hardly imaginable today.

Garlands like these are fiddly to make and require practice, but basically they are clusters of flowers bound around ribbon or string with fine wire – taking care to balance and distribute them evenly. They are worth trying, but remember that these subtle, steely colour combinations look wonderful in other ways too: similar hydrangeas mounded with plums on a verdigris platter look chic and understated with aubergine glass on the previous page and on an old blue-and-white china platter would look pretty and homely.

If the idea of garlands appeals but seems too complicated, try this idea of Constance Spry's, using exquisite garden roses laid simply on the table surface in baroque sweeping garlands or circlets around antique candelabra. Well-conditioned flowers easily last the duration of a dinner party and can be rearranged in water afterwards. These went on to last several days in a large bowl. Try pinks or sweet Williams for an inexpensive alternative version.

Sweeping garlands may look like the heavenly creations of a team of baroque cherubs but they are, in fact, simple to make. The cut roses were given a long drink, dried and simply placed in elegant curves on the table. The antique-looking English roses are 'Evelyn', 'Sweet Juliet', 'Jayne Austin', 'Abraham Darby', 'Sharifa Asma' and 'Heritage', and their delicate colours echo the marble candelabra.

Nerines and Rosehips

AUTUMN PARTY

There is indeed a harmony when flowers and setting are of a similar colour and this is particularly true of shades of red, which can seem harsh and strident in calmer environments. These particularly vibrant hues looked warm and inviting in this elegant red dining room with its ruby glass and firelight glow. The tall style of arrangement was inspired by the perpetual space problem of seating relatively small numbers of guests at long narrow tables. I made two arrangements in old iron three-tiered cakestands, which were positioned at each end of a particularly long table, leaving room for eight dinner guests to be seated facing each other in a cosier way.

The flowers were arranged into pre-soaked foam blocks firmly attached to each plate on the stands. I arranged the prickly rosehips first, then carefully positioned the flowers and covered the foam with mixed leaves. The aim was to keep the style light and quite wild, in keeping with the rosehips.

... there is a harmony

In autumn, and a lustre in its sky.

P.B. SHELLEY (1792–1822)

Simple metal cakestands filled with glowing three-tier arrangements of shimmering red hybrid nerines, rosehips and scarlet dahlias, all teamed with a rich collection of mixed autumn leaves including bergenia and beetroot with a few sprays of fuchsia and cotoneaster.

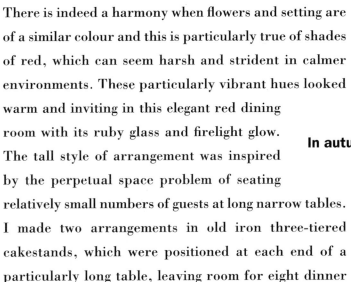

Mistletoe

A CHRISTMAS DINNER

Decorating modern rooms for Christmas offers an opportunity to create something fresh and unfussy while still observing seasonal traditions. Mistletoe was highly prized by Druids for its magical properties, which ranged from safeguarding against sorcery, lightning and thunderbolts to being a curative for ulcers, epilepsy and infertility. However, its potential could only be realized if it was never allowed to touch the earth – thus the custom of hanging it up at Christmas. Inspired by this, I suspended several healthy clumps of mistletoe with yacht wires above this large metal table, allowing them to reflect in its frozen surface. This icy feeling continued in the choice of brushed glass plates and steel cutlery, which were placed around a centrepiece glass bowl through which lichened branches of apple and mistletoe were interwoven. I then filled the bowl with water and floating candles to create a glowing and mystical cauldron.

A lavish canopy of mistletoe hanging from a bedroom gallery and underlit by a bowl of floating candles combines simplicity and drama with ancient winter traditions in this elegant modern apartment.

White Camellias

A QUIET WEDDING BREAKFAST

Single white camellias, extravagantly combined with heavily scented ivory gardenias on a frosted glass platter, create an image of utter luxury befitting a very special nuptial meal.

White flowers will always be a favourite choice for any wedding celebration.

In this glorious combination of white and ivory flowers, gardenias amply compensate for camellias' only downfall – their lack of scent. Otherwise, single camellias are rare perfection, especially when grown in a cool greenhouse to protect them from weather damage. They would be an excellent choice for a registry-office wedding bouquet – the perfect formal and sophisticated accessory for a classic cream Chanel suit. It would be rare to get enough camellia blooms like this to decorate several tables, and yet their formality makes them somewhat grand for everyday decoration. A single intimate formal table is therefore the perfect place to use them. As the petals of both gardenia and camellia bruise so easily, I cut the flowers delicately, split their stems and then arranged them straight into this bowl of water.

For a larger scale wedding, this polished and almost unreal perfection could be adapted – perhaps combining stephanotis, with its waxy fragrant flowers and glossy green leaves, with pale, fully open, bought roses. Alternatively, you could match the shining leaves of any camellia after it has flowered with open double white tulips in spring, or in summer the exquisite old rugosa rose 'Blanche Double de Coubert' would provide appearance and scent combined.

Celebrations

Armfuls of brilliant tulips with blue-and-white china.

Shimmering buttercups for a special anniversary.

Glowing harvest fruits on candlelit tables.

Fountains of jasmine for a white winter wedding.

Spring Meadow
CHRISTENING PARTY

In spring many exquisite plants are readily available in full flowering perfection.

It is the ideal time to use them in decorations such as the impressive buffet table for a christening celebration shown overleaf. A strong trestle table, protected by polythene, was covered with several turves of grass. Plants, still in pots, were arranged in sweeps of single varieties around them, and spaces and pots were then hidden with moss, pebbles and forest bark. Finally, pieces of ivy stapled to the table edge made a trailing woodland tablecloth. Food on plain creamware plates was arranged through the plants – rather like a smart picnic. The two other arrangements, shown on this page are quicker and easier alternatives that give the same impression of delicate spring freshness on a smaller scale. They would make ideal individual table arrangements with or without the meadow buffet table and, like it, provide a unique growing memento to share with friends and family afterwards.

Above: **White violets (Viola cucullata 'Alba'), yellow violas, sandwort (Arenaria montana) and Sedum acre planted in a china compote decorate a small side-table.**

Opposite: **Another growing arrangement of miniature border pinks (Dianthus 'Little Jock') edged with creeping Corsican mint (Mentha requienii).**

Overleaf: **A buffet table with a more elaborate interpretation of this delicate theme – a growing meadow of spring flowers, including bluebells, lily-of-the-valley, heartsease (Viola tricolor), saxifrage, cowslips, and violets.**

Parrot Tulips

A BIRTHDAY DINNER

The Tulip and the butterfly
Appear in gayer coats than I:
Let me be dressed fine as I will,
Flies, worms and flowers exceed me still.

ISAAC WATTS (1674–1748)

The rainbow colours of tulips are quite dazzling and the cut blooms almost arrange themselves – unless of course you prefer them strictly vertical. This is definitely not my preference, so I am always interested in containers that allow them to do their own thing. Tulips were chosen for this birthday party with a rather classical flavour, and the date and colour of the room prompted me to use Dutch china as containers. These delightful pots are copies of designs from the eighteenth-century days of Tulipomania when tulips were extremely expensive and could only be used in small quantities. (An idea of their worth can be gathered from the cautionary tale of the Dutch housekeeper, who fatefully mistook some highly prized tulip bulbs for onions and made them into soup – after her death the bulbs were valued at £1000.) These pots have lids with small holes, like some rose bowls, and support the sinuous stems perfectly. To allow them to curve so gracefully, they should be arranged a day, or even two, before a party. Combined with simple blue-edged china, and with magnificent *tulipières* – tall, tiered china pots that hold about 30 tulips – around the room the effect was bright, young and yet very much in keeping with the beautiful setting.

Red parrot tulips with canary featherings, yellow parrot tulips with red flashes, and single red and yellow striped tulips together make a brilliant splash in these square blue-and-white china pots.

Garden Leaves

SILVER WEDDING

This charming silver table decoration is a microcosm of a lush Renaissance garden – profusion within formality.

It can also be made in quantity without costing the earth. Miniature parterres were easily made from squares of cheap wood with dry floral foam glued in strips to make low 'hedges'. Small pieces of cut box (moss would do just as well) were then inserted into the foam and trimmed with scissors. Their formal shape hints perfectly at past glories while the silvery contents – all gleaned from the garden borders – tumble out and provide a subtle link with the celebration.

The idea of a central urn of garden roses could be elaborated upon by having a different type of rose on each table in various shades of silvery whites and purple-pinks. This both provides a wonderful talking point for dinner guests and contributes to a more relaxed and natural overall effect.

Miniature parterres for a silver wedding, overflowing with the purple and silvery foliage of ballota, euphorbia, *Rosa glauca*, silver acacia, eucalyptus, cotinus, lavender and *Stachys byzantina*.

A Bank of Buttercups

GOLDEN WEDDING

No flower is more golden than the buttercup, and if their flowering period coincides with this special anniversary, they are the perfect choice for a party. Though they are seldom cut for decoration, long-stemmed buttercups grow with abandon, last quite well and are considered a weed – so no one should

A glorious mass of golden buttercups – surprisingly sophisticated at close quarters – shimmers on this oak table for a golden wedding celebration.

mind you cutting them (though ask first). You do need to pick a good quantity, as a lot goes a little way, and allow them to drink in a cool spot overnight before arranging. Here I used shallow baking trays, filling them with a layer of moss-covered, pre-soaked floral foam. Then I inserted the stems liberally and casually to create a veritable field of shining golden flowers the length of the table. Simple, effective, and inexpensive.

Autumn Fruits

HARVEST BANQUET

The richest colours of autumn are combined in these sumptuous harvest celebration table decorations. Parties at this time of year are often more relaxed affairs than those leading up to Christmas, and these exuberant arrangements reflect that emphasis on fun and high spirits – definitely more barn-dancing than waltzing!

The ingredients (all recyclable!) for the long buffet table are simply laid straight on to the cloth in mounds of one type of fruit or vegetable, interspersed with cranberries in glass and pewter bowls. Lodged between fruits, well-conditioned branches of crab apple and other foliage last through the night quite happily without water. However, bowls of water or floral foam could easily be hidden beneath them if necessary. Individual tables are each given a bubbled glass bowl of crab apples. Their luxuriant garland is easily made using a pre-soaked foam ring shape and inserting small clumps of berries and foliage until it is covered. The bundles of miniature carrots, bound with wire hidden by a green stem of carrot foliage, are added last.

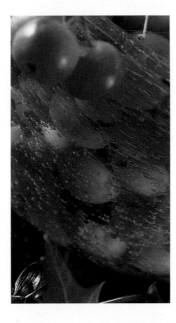

Overleaf: **A glorious mound of harvest fruits and vegetables piled on the dark green cloth of a long buffet table – sweetcorn, pumpkins, apples, crab apples and bowls of luscious cranberries all entwined with sedum, vines, maple leaves, hydrangeas, berberis and the neon-blue flowers of *Ceratostigma willmottianum*.**

Far left: **An individual table decorated with candlelit glass bowls of golden-red crab apples surrounded by harvest garlands.**

To load and bless
With fruit that round the thatch-eaves run;
To bend with apples the moss'd cottage-trees,
And fill with fruit with ripeness to the core.

JOHN KEATS (1795–1821)

Blue Roses

GOTHIC BALL

It was during the horror of a deep night…

JEAN RACINE (1639–1699)

The scene is set for a gothic ball, with the lilac-grey tones of the roses 'Little Silver' and 'Sterling Star' and the sombre mauve flowers of arum lilies, myrtle, wax flowers, ivy and lichened branches, all arranged like faded Victorian funeral tributes under glass domes.

The decoration for themed parties is in reality more like theatrical set design,

with over-the-top props, flowers and tableware setting the appropriate quirky tone. In this way, the theme is stated clearly and wittily from the moment guests arrive. The choice of location helps enormously – a dungeon, cellar or mysterious hall would be ideal here – but a lot can be done with clever use of fabric, candles and props. Flowers, too, can play their part. For this Gothic theme, I chose pallid and unhealthy shades of grey and lilac to give a moonlit, unsettling aura. The 'blue' roses were particularly appropriate, and looked suitably anaemic under glass domes – like funerary tributes from another age. Waxy arums and graveyard berries and ivy continue the ghostly feeling, all emphasized by flickering church candles and swirls of dry ice.

This arrangement is perfect for central buffet tables, while smaller tables echo the theme with ghostly flowers under domes or simple flickering candles alone.

Pastels
CHRISTMAS PARTY

A Christmas table with
a 'cherry tree' in a sparkling
urn as its magical centrepiece.
The theme of 'shimmery pastels'
continues with silvered apples
and tiny bowls of nerines.

This is a fresh contrast to all those sombre traditional Christmas tables laden with

evergreens and red fruits. Serious deviations from this norm are often portrayed as rather dubious in taste, but any seasonal idea – traditional or outrageous – has potential if part of a well thought-out scheme. This table has a childlike, magical quality completely appropriate to the season and works because the delicate, sparkling theme has been carried through fully and boldly – from the glittering centrepiece, through the bowls of shimmery nerines, to the metallic organza cloth and nightlights.

The basic ingredients are economical – important when several tables are planned. Tiny dried oak leaves were glued to some shapely branches of contorted hazel concreted into a small pot. The tree was roughly sprayed gold then silver for a tarnished effect, and silvered apples were strewn across the table. Placed in its glitter-filled glass urn and hung with deep red glâcé cherries, this enchanting shimmery tree is the stuff of fairytales.

Winter Jasmine

A WINTER WEDDING

Choice in flowers and colours for winter weddings is by nature limited. The reds and greens of Christmas look tired and jaded by New Year, while the vivid freshness of spring flowers or the summery hues of the lilies and roses now available all year around can look tawdry and brash. At this time of year, jasmine plants in full flower are widely available, and their soft, scented trails bring an elegant refinement to such special celebrations. With their shining mass of whiteness blushed with

Plants that wake whilst others sleep
Timid jasmine buds that keep
Their fragrance to themselves all day,
But when the sunlight dies away
Let their delicious secret out
To every breeze that roams about.

THOMAS MOORE (1779–1852)

pink, they look wonderful planted in and spilling from interesting containers of all sorts. For this occasion, however, I wanted to create a lighter, flowing shower of blossom and improvized this two-tier arrangement by placing a glass flute vase on to a stemmed bowl. Flowering sprays were then snipped off the market-bought plants and arranged directly into the water-filled fountain (proper conditioning would damage the delicate flowers). The plants could later be given to wedding guests to enjoy.

The spicy and delicious scent of shell-white jasmine flowers (*Jasminum polyanthum*) fills the air for a wedding in the dull days of late winter.

A delicate fountain of jasmine in the middle of each table exquisitely marries elegance to simplicity. The plain crystal champagne flutes, tall glass candlesticks and finely embroidered cloth all combine to emphasize the lightness and refinement of the whole scheme.

Some Practical Points

MAKING FLOWERS LAST LONGER

There are many factors that govern the lasting power of cut flowers. By their nature, flowers are ephemeral pleasures, but I do advocate several simple rules to ensure that one has at least done one's best to keep them looking good. Most importantly, as with most things, choosing the highest quality is the best starting point. Whenever you buy flowers, examine them for bruising, wilting leaves or slimy stems – all signs of rough handling and age. It is also best to avoid having fully open blooms on most flowers.

If you are cutting flowers or foliage yourself, try to pick them during the coolest part of the day or in the evening and avoid leaving the stems lying in the sun waiting to be collected. Cut flowers – whether bought from a shop or picked from the garden – should seldom be arranged straight away. Whatever you buy or cut, it is essential to recut the stems immediately before putting them into water. It is also worth taking the time to condition them properly. This rather off-putting word is a collective term for several basic common-sense procedures. You may be irritated that you have to wait a while before you can enjoy your flowers, but I would reassure the sceptic that they will last longer than usual if treated properly. Here are the most useful conditioning points to bear in mind:

Recut stems immediately, then put flowers into buckets of water, and leave them to drink in a cool place for as long as possible, preferably overnight. (*Only very delicate or open flowers such as camellia, gardenia or jasmine do not benefit from this and should be arranged directly.*)

Remove leaves which will be below water, otherwise they will decay.

For flowers with hard or woody stems, such as roses and shrubs, hammer or split the bottom few centimetres of stem with scissors before putting into water.

For flowers with hollow stems, such as amaryllis, which often get air bubbles, make a small vertical cut in the stem just below the flowerhead to release trapped air. For delphiniums remove the top bud.

Flowers with more foliage than blossom, such as lilac and bride's blossom (philadelphus), last longer and look prettier if most of the leaves are removed. The stems seem unable to drink enough water for both leaves and flowers and everything soon wilts if left in place.

For flowers with milky sap, such as hellebores, place the cut stem in a few centimetres of boiling water and allow to cool. Hellebores then seem to enjoy being submerged in cool water for a few hours – this should also revive them if they wilt. Hydrangeas also enjoy this treatment; bluebells, poppies and lilac all benefit from initial boiling without submerging.

If stems wilt, re-cut the bottom and place in deep warm water. If this fails, repeat with a few centimetres of boiling water.

Remember that bulbs and growing plants are usually accustomed to cooler outside conditions. Keep them watered but never wet (read individual care instructions) and replant bulbs in the garden when the flowering is over.

A drop of bleach seems to keep water clean (particularly useful for glass containers), but I find sugar, aspirin or plant food do little for longevity.

Finally, place the completed arrangement away from sources of extreme heat or cold and top up with water regularly.

THE FLORAL FOAM VERSUS CHICKEN WIRE DEBATE

I have been purposefully vague about mechanics in this book – that is, supporting bits and pieces. It is a question of individual preference and suitability of container. I prefer to use containers in the home which do not need either floral foam or chicken wire, and certainly for the arrangements in this book, weight of stem is seldom a problem. If, however, your flowers need some extra support, light use of wire or floral foam is all that is needed (the latter secured to your container with tape or reel wire). I personally avoid using floral foam with soft stemmed or spring flowers.

Index

acacia 108
agapanthus 43, 78
alliums, purple-black 40
amaryllis 48-9, 124
Arenaria montana 101
Arum italicum 21
arum lilies 116
asparagus fern 89
astrantia, variegated 36
auriculas 22-3
Autumn 44-6, 89-93, 112-15

ballota 108
bedding plants 24
beetroot 93
berberis 113
bergenia 93
berries 44-5, 112-13
birthdays 58-9, 89, 104-7
blackcurrants 36
blossom 61-3
bluebells 66, 101, 124
box 108
breakfast 40-1
bride's blossom 124
buffet tables 116
bulbs 124
    crocus 18-19
    snowdrops 16-17
buttercups 110-11

cacti 84-5
camellias 14-15, 21, 96-7, 124
    'Black Lace' 14
    white 12
candles 70, 73, 80, 88, 94, 116
carnations 89
catkins 62
celebrations 99-125
Centranthus ruber 39
Ceratostigma willmottianum 113
Chaenomeles 14-15
cherry blossom 61-3
chestnuts 46
chicken wire 39, 56, 62, 124

Chimonanthus praecox 15
Chinese witch hazel 15
chives 66
Christening party 100-1
Christmas 50-1, 94-5, 118-19
chrysanthemums 43
Clematis 66
    montana 64-5
    wild 46
conditioning 124
containers
    bamboo 87
    baskets 26, 72
    bowls
        etched green glass 14-15
        frosted glass 10
        marble 56
        mosaic 33
        terracotta 36
    brass platter 89
    cake ring 16-17
    cake stand 93
    cobalt blue 43, 53
    decanters 20
    glass bottles 34-5, 43
    glass domes 116
    glasses
        antique 20
        champagne 70
    growing plants 22, 24, 124
    ink pot 30
    oriental 62, 87
    pestle 22-3, 34
    soup tureens 66
    stone 84
    terracotta 36, 40
    trays
        baking 111
        metal 19, 89
    tulipières 104
    vases
        curved 12
        painted 78
cornflowers 43
Cornus mas 48-9

Corsican mint 101
cotinus 108
cotoneaster 93
cowslip 101
crocus 18-19

dahlias 93
damsons 45, 82
Daphne odora 15, 21
delphiniums 78-9, 124
Dianthus 'Little Jock' 101
dinner parties 56-7, 80-1,
    86-7, 92-5
drinks parties 60-1, 70-1,
    72-3, 82-3

Easter blossom 60-1
echeveria 33
echinops 43
elderberries 45
English roses 40-1, 72-3, 90-1
eryngium 43
eucalyptus 108
euphorbia 36, 89, 108

fennel 33, 36
feverfew 36
floral foam
    in arrangements 45, 62, 72,
        82, 93, 108
    v. chicken wire 124
flowers
    conditioning 124
    meanings 39
    position on table 7
foliage
    arrangement 36-7
    autumn 93, 113
    chestnuts 46
    Christmas 119
    with fruit 82
    parterres 108-9
    with roses 33, 40
    skeletonized leaves 50-1
forget-me-nots 43

forsythia 62
fountains 87
fraises des bois 33, 75
fruit
    autumn 45
    'cherry tree' 118-19
    currants 36, 82-3
    damsons 45, 82
    greengages 82
    harvest celebration 113-15
    lemons 53
    pears 51-2
    plums 89
    sloes 45
    strawberries 33, 75-7
fuchsia 93

gardenia 97, 124
garlands 50-1, 80-1, 89-91, 113
gentians 44-5
Geranium 24, 66
    robertianum 39
golden philadelphus 36
golden wedding 110-11
grapes 45
grass turves 101-2
gravel 17
greengages 82
guelder roses 10-11

Hamamelis mollis 15
harvest celebration 113-15
heartsease 101
Helleborus 20-1, 124
    corsicus 21
    foetidus 21
    orientalis 21
Helxine 19
herb robert 39
Hermodactylus tuberosus 12-13
Heuchera 'Palace Purple' 40
hollyhocks 78-9
    'Black Prince' 78
honeysuckle 36, 39
Hosta 36

hyacinths 10–11
   Roman 53–4
hydrangeas 46, 88–9, 113, 124

Iris 'Pauline' 21
ivy 116

Japanese influences 15, 62, 86–7
Japanese quince 14
jasmine 120–2, 124
Jasminium polyanthum 121

lavender 43, 108
leaves *see* foliage
leis 81
lemon balm 36
lemons 53
Lenten rose 20–1
light 6, 43, 45
lilac 66–7, 124
lilies 21, 34, 43, 116
lily-of-the-valley 30–1, 101
Linard, Jacques 22
Lotus 80–1
   orem ipsem plantum 81
lunches 43, 65, 66, 78

magnolias 56–7
maple leaves 46, 113
marigolds 81
Mentha requienii 101
mind-your-own-business 19
mistletoe 94–5
moss 24, 58, 62, 108, 111
Mother's Day 10–11
Muguet 30
Muscari comosum
   'Plumosum' 66
myrtle 116

Narcissus 58–9
   'Paper White' 58
   'Tête-â-Tête' 58
   white 12, 53
nasturtiums 81

nerines 92–3, 119
nicotianas 24, 78
nuts, chestnuts 46

orchids 86–7
Ornithogalum arabicum 12–13
outdoor meals 36–7, 72–3, 74–7

pears 51–2
penstemon 43
perovskia 43
petunias 24
Phalaenopsis 87
Philadelphus 75–7, 124
   'Belle Etoile' 75
   'Burfordensis' 75
   coronarius 'Aureus' 36
Phytolacca americana 45
picnics 75–7
pinks 90, 100–1
plums 89
Polianthes tuberosa 81
poppies 124
Portugal laurel 53
primroses 58
   double 24–5
primulas 24
privet berries 45
Prunus
   lusitanica 53–4
   padus 62

quince, Japanese 14

ranunculus 26–7
red valerian 39
Rhododendron 66
   'Chrismas Cheer' 21
Roman hyacinths 53–4
rosehips 92–3
rosemary 53
roses (*Rosa*) 32–6
   conditioning 124
   English 40–1, 72–3, 90–1
   garlands 90

miniature 24
old 39
silver weddings 108
white 34–5
yellow 72–3
R. glauca 108
R. mundi 39
R. officinalis 39
R. rugosa 97, 108
R. wichuraiana hybrid 34
var. 'Abraham Darby' 90
var. 'Blanche Double de
   Coubert' 97
var. 'Chapeau de Napoléon' 39
var. 'Charles Rennie
   Mackintosh' 40
var. 'Charlotte' 72
var. 'Cymbeline' 40
var. 'English Garden' 72
var. 'Evelyn' 90
var. 'Glamis Castle' 34
var. 'Golden Celebration' 72
var. 'Henri Martin' 39
var. 'Heritage' 90
var. 'Jayne Austin' 90
var. 'La Reine Victoria' 39
var. 'Little Silver' 116
var. 'Louise Odier' 39
var. 'Madame Alfred
   Carrière' 33
var. 'Old Blush China' 39
var. 'Sharifa Asma' 90
var. 'Sterling Star' 116
var. 'Sweet Juliet' 90
rue 33

St Valentine's Day 16–17
sand 84
sandwort 101
saxifrage 101
scabious 78
seasonal flowers 6
Sedum 33, 82, 113
   acre 101
shells 46

silver wedding 108–9
simple arrangements 9–54
single-flower arrangements 42–3
sloes 45
snowdrops 16–17
Spring 10–20, 24–31, 56–65, 101
Stachys byzantina 108
stephanotis 53, 97
stones 19
strawberries 75–7
   miniature 33
Summer 33–43, 66–86
sunflowers 34
suppers 44–5, 52–3
sweet peas 43, 70–1
sweet Williams 90

tuberose 81
tulip tree, leaves 46
tulips 28–9, 97, 104–7
Turkish chincherinchees 12–13
twigs 48, 94, 116, 119

vegetables 45, 113–15
viburnum berries 45
vines 113
Viola 24
   cucullata 'Alba' 101
   tricolor 101
   yellow 101
violets 26, 90, 101
Virginian pokeweed berries 45

wax flowers 116
weddings 97, 120–2
   anniversaries 89, 108–9,
   110–11
whitecurrants 82–3
widow iris 12–13
willow 62
Winter 21, 48–53, 118–22
wintersweet 15
witch hazel, Chinese 15

zinnias 81

Author's acknowledgments

Putting this book together has been an enormous pleasure and I am greatly indebted to the many people who helped to make it that way: most importantly to Jan Baldwin who made every photography session a total joy with her unique blend of technical prowess, creative intuitions and calm good humour. Our names on the front cover should be joined by two others: Louise Simpson, who commissioned this book in the first place and was always the most patient and diplomatic of editors, and Leslie Harrington – art editor par excellence – whose humour and enthusiasm is matched only by her skill and artistic genius. My thanks are due also to Lucinda Egerton who found such perfect props to enhance the flowers and so patiently endured my interference at all stages; to Jenna Jarman who stage-managed the creative processes and edited the final manuscripts and to the whole Conran Octopus production and publicity teams for making the book possible and including me so much at every stage.

I was very fortunate in having such exquisite flowers to arrange for these photographs and my sincere thanks are due to those who supplied them: – to Christine Corson whose boxes of treasures from her garden in Dorset were, like her, a delight and inspiration (my thanks also to Lady Harmsworth who so willingly chauffeured them to London); to David Austin who let me loose in his beautiful rose garden in Wolverhampton and who, together with his wife and staff, was always so helpful and encouraging; to my suppliers at Covent Garden market: David Gortin at A & F Bacon Ltd; Dick at C. Gardiner Ltd; Alan and Stella at Alagar; Teddy at Page Monro; Edward at C. M. Grover Ltd; John at Arnott and Mason Ltd.; Bill and Bobby at L. Mills and Adam and Steve at H. Miles Ltd.

I am greatly indebted to those friends and clients who let us use their homes for photography: my dear friend Sylvia Cooper who gave her home (with delicious lunches) on two occasions; Simon and Lucinda Fraser; Mr and Mrs Tom Egerton; Bob Baldwin; Mrs Bowden-Cumming; Mr and Mrs Alasdair Simpson; Andrew Mortada; Mr and Mrs Eric Wetter de Sanchez; Rushka Scorr-Kern; and Mr Allen and Dr Susanna Everitt. I am particularly indebted to Kate Dyson who lent us many exquisite and covetable treasures from the *Dining Room Shop* (64, White Hart Lane, London SW13, 0181 878 1020) and was always so enthusiastic and encouraging; similarly to Bridget Bodrano at the *Conran Shop* (Fulham Road, London SW3, 0171 589 7401) and to the following individuals whose props made the photographs complete: *Tom Morgan*; *General Trading Co.* (144 Sloane Street, London SW1X, 0171 730 0411); *Graham and Green* (4/7 Elgin Crescent, London W11, 0171 727 4594); *Sam Wade*; *Viaduct Furniture Ltd.* (1-10 Sumners Street, London EC1); *Michael and*

Carol Francis Ceramics (Llandre, Llanfyrnach, Crymych, Dyfed, Wales SA 35, 01239 831657); David and Charles Wainwright (61, Portobello Road, London W11, 0171 727 0707); and Nicholas Haslam (12, Holbein Place, London SW1, 0171 730 8623).

Finally my special personal thanks to those who have been the backstage support system. Most importantly to "the team" – Tracy Elson (and the Tracemobile); Nigel Watts; Sharon Melehi and their respective partners who together make it all possible and, more importantly, all enjoyable; also to Cynthia Woods and Jo Bogan; to those who have inspired and guided: Michael Goulding O.B.E. and Elizabeth Barker M.B.E.; Sheila Quaddy; and Caroline Evans; and lastly to my friends and family – especially to my father-in-law, Robin Denniston – not least for his contractual advice, to my mother (who still arranges flowers better than me) and father for always supporting and encouraging me, and to my wife Candida for typing, reading, comforting, calming and generally making everything worthwhile.